GIFTS OF GOD

HOPE

JOEL OSTEEN

CONTENTS

INTRODUCTION

Hope is a powerful gift from God!

In Jeremiah 29:11, God declares, "'*For I know the plans I have for you,' says the Lord. 'They are plans for good and not for disaster, to give you a future and a hope*'" (NLT).

Hope is much greater than you may have ever realized — it's more than an emotion or feeling. Hope is an amazing gift that God wants you to experience every moment of every day.

Maybe you've put your hope in your career, a friend or perhaps a family member. It's something we've all done and can lead to pain and disappointment.

But the solution isn't found in letting go of hope. It's found by putting your hope in the right place.

David wrote in Psalm 71:5, *"O Lord, You alone are my hope"* (NLT). David had been through tough times in his life when he wrote those words.

Yet through it all, he realized this truth: It's only in God that we can put our hope.

In the following pages, you're going to discover this truth in a greater way. No matter what your past may look like or the circumstances that surround you, God still has a plan for your life, and it will come to pass.

So as you read, ask God to show you the areas of your life where you need hope. And believe that with Him, all things are possible.

Get ready to experience His hope in your life every day.

CHAPTER ONE

GOD'S TIMING

GOD HAS A GIFT FOR YOU,
AND IT'S A LIFE FILLED
WITH HOPE!

YOUR TIME IS COMING

God has put promises, dreams and desires in every one of our hearts.

But so often we give up before the promises come to pass. Maybe we tried and failed too many times, or someone didn't treat us right in the process.

It can be easy to get complacent or discouraged and find a reason to stop pursuing what God has put in your heart. But I want to encourage you to get your fire back.

God has a gift for you, and it's a life filled with hope!

No matter how long it's been, no matter how impossible it looks, as you stay in faith, your time is going to come.

Every dream that's in your heart, every promise that has taken root, God put them there, and He has every intention of bringing them to pass.

May this be your declaration: "My time is coming. I've been believing and obeying. I haven't seen a lot of results yet, but that's okay . . . I know my time is coming."

Or, "We're living in a small apartment now, but my family is growing. I'm not discouraged. I know our time is coming."

Or, "I really want to get married. I haven't met the right person yet, but I know God's in control. At the right time, He's going to make it happen. My time is coming."

That's what hope is all about — believing the promises God put in you will come to pass.

I love what David said: *"I've pitched my tent in the land of hope"* (Acts 2:26, MSG). So let me ask you — where have you pitched your tent? What are you expecting each day? What kind of attitude do you have?

Maybe for years you have been praying for a wayward child. You're afraid they're never going to change. Or maybe all your co-workers are being promoted but not you. Perhaps you tried to start a business, but no one would invest in your dream.

It's in those moments you've got to turn away from negative thoughts and disappointments. If you don't, you'll pitch your tent in the wrong place. You'll settle in a land that doesn't expect God's blessings and favor.

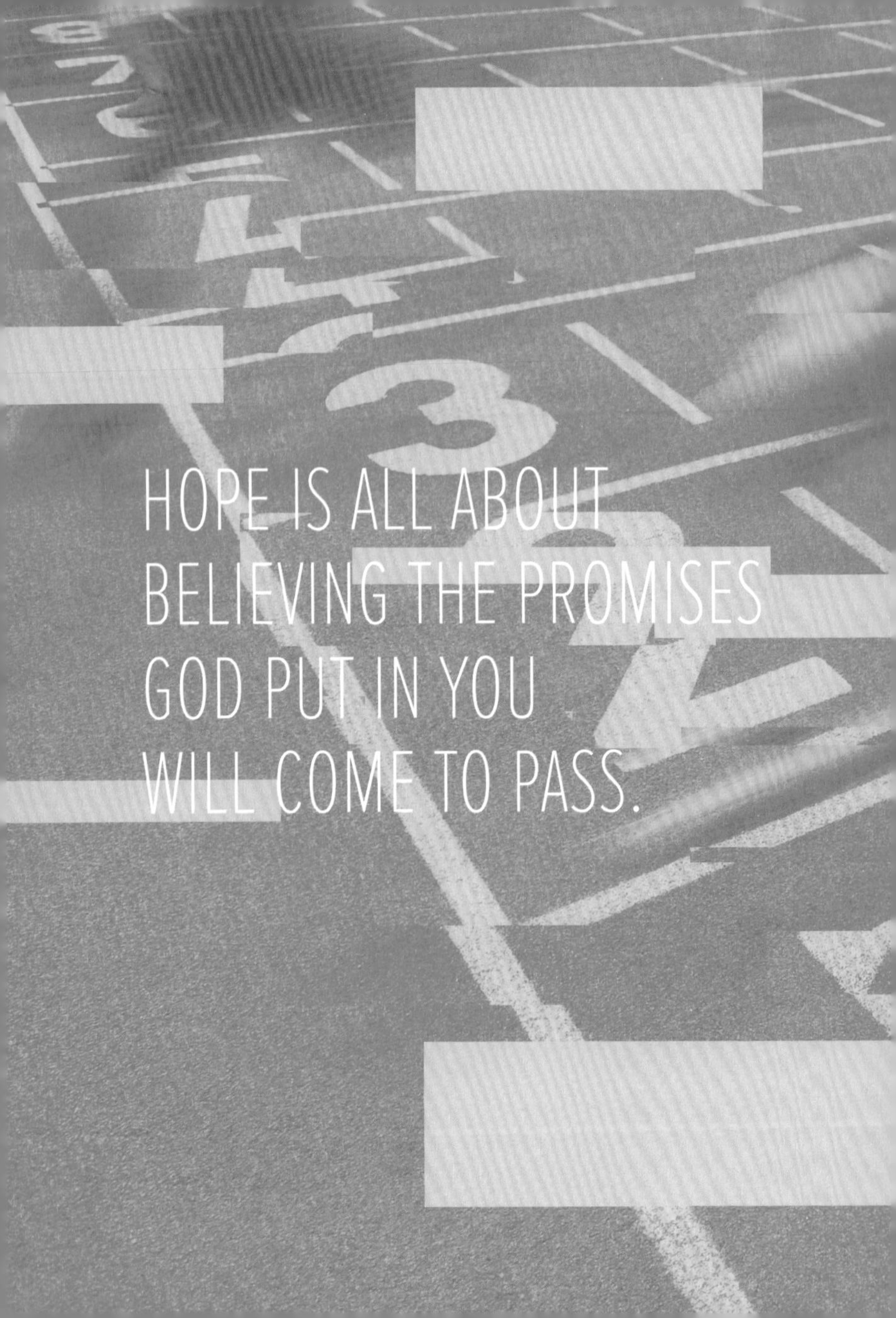

HOPE IS ALL ABOUT
BELIEVING THE PROMISES
GOD PUT IN YOU
WILL COME TO PASS.

LIVE A LIFE OF EXPECTANCY

A clear way to determine what land you're in is to ask yourself, "Do I believe God can turn this around? Do I believe He will?"

If you don't believe He will and aren't expecting Him to move on your behalf, then you need to go dig up your stakes, pack up your belongings, and move out of the land of discouragement.

Move into the land of hope, the land of faith, the land where you know anything is possible. The place where you know your time is coming because you're holding on to God's gift of hope.

Sometimes we just need to hear God's Word spoken over our lives.

Reading the Word reveals so much hope, but there are moments when we also need to hear the Word in order to grab ahold of those promises and make them our own.

You may need someone to help jump-start your faith, to breathe new life into your dreams. You may have been through countless disappointments and need encouragement to keep dreaming.

In the natural, you might have every reason to give up on what God's put in your heart.

But I'm asking you to let this simple phrase take root in your soul: *My time is coming*.

God is in control of your life. He knows exactly where you are, and He knows the hidden dreams He's put in you. The Scripture calls them the secret petitions of the heart — the things you haven't told anyone about.

Maybe you thought they would never work out, or you buried them because they didn't happen on your timeline. Be confident of this today: God still has a way to bring them to pass.

Declare today, "That's it. I'm done being complacent. I'm done settling for mediocrity. I'm going to believe that every dream, every promise and every secret petition of my heart is coming to fulfillment."

When you get up in the morning, tempted to be discouraged with negative thoughts telling you, "It's never going to happen. You're never going to get married. You're never going to get out of debt. You're never going to be happy. This is as good as it gets . . ."

Shake off that thinking and pray:

> "Father, You said the path of the righteous gets brighter and brighter. You said no good thing will You withhold because I walk uprightly. You said because I delight myself in You, You would give me the secret petitions of my heart. So Father, I thank You that You're in control of my life. Good things are in store, and I believe my time is coming."

As you stay in an attitude of faith and expectancy, you're going to see God make your dreams come to pass.

DOUBLE YOUR RETURN

When you go through an unfair circumstance, and we all do, I want to encourage you not to make the mistake of constantly dwelling on it. Let it go. Let that hurt, anger and pain roll off your back.

Too many people have pitched their tents in the land of self-pity. Somebody mistreated them years ago, and instead of it challenging them for a moment, that hurt defined them for a lifetime.

And after all this time, they're still allowing it to poison their lives.

But the Scripture says in Zechariah 9:12, *"Come back to the place of safety, all you prisoners who still have hope! I promise this very day that I will repay two blessings for each of your troubles"* (NLT).

That means if somebody does you wrong, instead of getting negative and bitter, have an

"COME BACK TO THE PLACE OF SAFETY, ALL YOU PRISONERS WHO STILL HAVE HOPE! I PROMISE THIS VERY DAY THAT I WILL REPAY TWO BLESSINGS FOR EACH OF YOUR TROUBLES."

ZECHARIAH 9:12, NLT

attitude that says, "They just did me a favor. They just qualified me for double. And I'm going to believe my time is coming and come out with twice the joy, twice the peace and twice the victory."

That's what an attitude of hope looks like. An attitude that says, "I will not be defeated. It may look impossible, but I know God makes all things possible. They may have treated me wrong, but I'm not worried. I know God is my Vindicator. It may be taking a long time, but in due season, I know I will reap if I just don't give up."

This is what Joseph did. He spent thirteen years in prison for something he didn't do. Yet Joseph was faithful; he kept being good to people and having a good attitude.

How could he have possibly not become bitter? Joseph understood that his time was coming.

Maybe, like Joseph, you have been through a series of losses. It hasn't felt like life has treated you fair. You've begun thinking, "It's never going to get any better. This is just my lot in life."

If you're not careful, your bad attitudes and negative thoughts could make your challenges that much more difficult.

We may start in one unfair situation, but then we perpetuate it by having the wrong mindset, making one small obstacle shipwreck our lives for years.

But you can begin a new attitude today. You can hold on to God's gift of hope.

You may have been through unfair situations. But it's not over until God says it's over. He always has the final say. He is a God of justice, and He sees every wrong ever done to you.

God is saying today, "If you will stay in faith, if you will keep your hopes up, I will turn your wrongs into rights. I will bring justice to your life. Your time is coming!"

CHAPTER TWO

LIVING EXAMPLES

BELIEVE YOU'RE GOING TO SEE MORE AND MORE OF GOD'S GOODNESS. BELIEVE YOU'RE GOING TO SEE GOD TURN THINGS AROUND. BELIEVE YOU'RE GOING TO SEE GOD OPEN UP NEW DOORS.

DON'T LET LIFE CHANGE YOUR NAME

I am so thankful for God's Word and the stories of faith I find there — the great men and women of faith whose struggles show us how we can live our lives in hope and victory.

One of these stories is about a lady named Naomi, which means "pleasant." So when everyone said, "Hello, Naomi," they were actually saying, "Hello, pleasant."

She was a pleasant woman with a sweet spirit everyone loved.

But Naomi went through a series of losses. Her husband died, and then her sons were killed. All these negative things came against her, and she made the mistake of letting her spirit fill with bitterness. She got soured on life.

Her attitude was, "All my dreams have been shattered. I'm never going to be happy. Just leave me in my heartache and misery." But of course, that was not God's plan for her.

Yes, it's difficult when we go through a time of loss. There's a proper time for grieving. We just can't let a season of mourning turn into a lifetime of mourning.

Naomi became so bitter she actually changed her name to Mara, which means "bitter." So when somebody said, "Hey, Naomi. How are you?" In essence, she said, "Don't call me that anymore because I'm no longer pleasant — there's nothing good in my life. I don't have any joy or hope. Call me by my new name: Mara."

Yet every time someone called her Mara, they were simply reminding her of her heartache, pain and the choice she made to be bitter. But God didn't forget her first name, and with some encouragement, the Bible shows us that Naomi gave up her bitterness. Her life was made pleasant again.

Here's the point I'm trying to share with you: *Don't let life change your name.*

You may have been through some unfair situations. Maybe one of your dreams has died.

Let me assure you that God still has a great plan for your life.

When one door closes, God will always open up a different one. Dig your heels in and say, "I may have been through a lot, but I've come too far to stop now. I refuse to get bitter. I refuse to live my life negatively. I know God has great things in store."

GOD'S GOODNESS IS AHEAD

What was the difference between Joseph and Naomi?

Joseph knew, even though life wasn't fair and had dealt him some tough blows, his time was coming. He pitched his tent in the land of hope.

I love the way the Amplified Bible translates David's words in Psalm 27:13: *"[What would have become of me] had I not believed that I would see the Lord's goodness . . ."* (AMP)!

In other words, no matter what comes your way, let the words of David take root in your heart. See them for what they really are — not just the words of a man, but the Word of God.

Believe you're going to see more and more of God's goodness. Believe you're going to see

God turn things around. Believe you're going to see God open up new doors.

I've learned that when you feel like dying, you need to talk about living. When you feel like giving up, talk about pressing forward. When you don't see any way out, talk about how God can make a way.

The enemy always fights you the hardest when he knows God has something great in store.

So when the bottom falls out, when it looks like you've hit an all-time low and things couldn't get any worse, hold on to hope. You don't know what God has around the corner.

When you face challenges in your life, don't focus on the negative and get bitter. Instead, put your shoulders back and boldly declare,

"My time is coming. I am a victor and not a victim. Today, I am choosing God's gift of hope."

I read about a man who went out sailing alone on his boat. It was a beautiful day, but before long, a huge storm came. The wind and waves crashed against his vessel, and eventually, his boat capsized. He barely survived and washed up on a deserted island.

Week after week went by, and he was so miserable, so distraught. He didn't think he would ever be found. He prayed and prayed, but it seemed like the Heavens were silent. Nothing got any better.

In fact, just when he thought it couldn't get any worse, after he was out one day trying to find some food, he came back to his camp and noticed the little, thatched roof hut he built had somehow caught on fire.

He just sat there and watched it go up in flames. It was like pouring salt on his wounds. He said, "God, I give up. I asked You to help me, but one bad thing after another keeps happening to me." He was so discouraged.

But about an hour later the Coast Guard showed up to rescue him. He couldn't believe it. He was thrilled! He said, "How in the world did you find me?" They said, "We saw the smoke coming from the fire you built."

My point is, if you feel like your "hut" is on fire, instead of getting negative and bitter, embrace a different perspective. Get a bigger view and believe that God is going to somehow,

someway, turn that around and use it to your advantage.

You may feel like Naomi; you feel like your life's been put on hold and so much has come against you. Things just aren't working out, and you're struggling with negative thoughts like, *It's never going to change. It's never going to get any better. You're never going to get well. You're never going to be happy.*

Friend, don't believe the "never" lies. God is saying, "Hold on to My gift of hope. Your time is coming."

CHAPTER THREE

STAY IN FAITH

“SO LET’S NOT GET TIRED OF DOING WHAT IS GOOD. AT JUST THE RIGHT TIME WE WILL REAP A HARVEST OF BLESSING IF WE DON’T GIVE UP.”

GALATIANS 6:9, NLT

GOD HOLDS YOUR DESTINY

When we are in the middle of a series of disappointments, we can forget that God is able to transform any situation. But the storm could be raging, and suddenly God calls out, "Peace, be still," and everything changes.

Joseph waited thirteen years. The dreams God had given him looked impossible. From the world's point of view, he didn't have a chance. But God still had a plan.

Even in prison, when Joseph was good to people and they said they would help him, when they got out, they forgot all about him.

Maybe you were counting on somebody to give you a break. You went out of your way to help someone succeed, but when you needed help, they were nowhere to be found.

Understand that ultimately, your destiny is not tied to people. Don't be discouraged because somebody walked away. Don't be bitter toward a boss, a business associate or a friend who got promoted and forgot about you. Your success isn't dependent on them.

God already has the right people lined up. He already has your divine connections. Just stay in faith; God will get you to where you need to be.

In the Bible, there was a man by the name of Simeon (Luke 2:25-26). One day God told him, "You will not die until you see the Christ."

He didn't understand how that promise would come to pass, but he let it take root deep down on the inside. He didn't tell anybody about it. It was just between him and God. And some commentaries say that he waited up to twenty years.

I can imagine the older he got the more he was tempted to think, "I must not have heard God right. It's never going to happen. It's been so many years."

No, Simeon had to do the same thing every person has to do when faced with difficult odds. When those negative thoughts came, he had to shake them off and declare, "No, my time is coming. The promise is in me. God put it in my heart, and I will not go to my grave until I see it fulfilled. I'm choosing hope."

He got up every morning hoping, believing and expecting. Sure enough, some twenty years later, he saw that promise come to pass.

IT WILL COME TO PASS

I believe God has spoken something like that to everyone. Maybe deep down on the inside, you have dreams that you know are going to come to pass before you leave this earth.

It's good to just remind God. Tell Him, "God, You put the promise in me that 'as for me and my house we will serve the Lord,' and I believe I will not go to my grave until I see my whole family serving You."

Maybe God's put a promise in you that one day you'll get married, but you've been through some disappointing and broken relationships. You're getting a little older, and you're being tempted to think it's not going to happen. No, God's already got the right person picked out, and you're never too old.

Maybe God's put a promise in you that one day you're going to write a book, one day you're going to be in management, one day you're going to have a successful business or one day you're going to have a ministry.

Yet right now, like Simeon, everything is trying to tell you why it's not going to happen. "Oh, you don't have the right connections. You've made too many mistakes."

Sometimes, the more we believe and the more we pray, the less likely it looks. It's easy to give in or give up, but instead, do what Simeon did.

No matter how long it's been, no matter how tempted you are to get discouraged, get up every morning and just declare by faith, "My time is coming. The promise is in me, and I will not die until I see it come to pass."

KEEP SOWING SEED

People tell me, "Well, Joel, I've been giving. I've been tithing my income for ten years. But I still don't see anything happening in my finances." I believe God is saying to you, "Stay faithful. Your time is coming."

"Well, I've been working at this job for twenty years, showing up early, giving it my best. And I still never get promoted." Don't get bitter. Don't be negative. You're not working unto man; you're working unto God.

If you'll keep the right attitude, your time of promotion will come. God is keeping the records. He sees every seed you've ever sown, and what you sow, you will reap!

Psalm 126:5 tells us those who sow in tears will reap in joy. That means the sowing seasons are usually the most difficult, and it can be hard to keep a good attitude when you seem to be the only one not being blessed.

It doesn't seem to make sense.

But times of waiting are only times of testing. It's hard to go through disappointments, to have people do us wrong; but stay positive and hopeful, and be good back to them.

These are seasons of sowing. And if you'll do the right thing, when you sow in tears, you will always reap in joy.

This is also a great opportunity for you to check your attitude.

Understand, we don't obey so God will bless us — we obey because we love Him.

If Simeon were standing before us today, he'd say, "Don't give up on that promise. Your

time is coming. Keep obeying God in faith. Keep choosing His gift of hope."

You need to let that sink deep down inside you. It's never too late. God is saying, "This is your season. Keep trusting Me, keep hoping and keep your faith strong."

CHAPTER FOUR

BELIEVE AGAIN

MERCY COUNTS
US IN! IT DOESN'T
COUNT US OUT.

GOD NEVER GIVES UP ON A DREAM

God had put a dream in Caleb that he would inhabit the Promised Land.

When he and Joshua were young men, they went and spied out the Promised Land with ten others. They came back and told Moses, "We are well able to take the land. Let us go in at once." But the other ten spies said just the opposite and didn't get to see the Promised Land.

I can imagine Caleb was discouraged. He knew they were supposed to go in. God put that dream in his heart, but it didn't happen. It looked like his time wasn't going to come.

Forty years went by, and it looked like he was done at the age of eighty-five. It seemed like the promise was over; but understand, God never aborts a dream, and Caleb hadn't forgotten either.

In the end, he moved into the land. His dream came to pass.

MERCY COUNTS US IN

You may be thinking, "Joel, you don't know what I've done. You don't know the life I've lived. You don't know the people I've hurt." That may be true, but nothing you've done is too much for the mercy of God.

If you get knocked down, all you've got to do is get back up again.

I love the fact that God's mercy doesn't count us out. It counts us in.

If you've ever watched a boxing match where one of the boxers gets knocked down, the referee comes over and counts, "One, two, three . . ." all the way up to "eight, nine, ten. You're out. You're done. You're disqualified."

But God's mercy is just the opposite.

When we get knocked down, when we make a mistake, God comes over and counts, "Ten, nine, eight . . ." all the way down to "three, two, one, zero."

But He doesn't shout, "You're out." He says, "All right. Get back up. It's time to begin again." Mercy counts us in! It doesn't count us out.

As you read this, your time may not be coming, because it is already here. You've sown into so many others. You've been faithful day in and day out. Just like Joseph, you did the right thing when the wrong thing was happening. And today, God is saying, "It's your time now. You're entering into a new season."

You may have had a lot of great things happen in the past, but you haven't seen anything new yet. Your best days are not behind you. They are ahead of you!

Maybe for you, it's going to be a new season of increase, a new season of promotion, a new season of blessing. For others, it's going to be a time of vindication, a time when God is going to make wrongs right.

Maybe, like He did for Joseph, God's going to bring justice into your life. It's going to be a time of supernatural strength when you'll break addictions, break bad habits and break wrong mindsets.

Maybe it's going to be a time when those hidden dreams you've had buried for years will start coming to pass.

God will open up new opportunities at the right time. He'll bring the right people across your path. As you're faithful, as you're a prisoner of hope, He'll take you into a new season of victory.

Whatever the disappointments, heartache or pain you've gone through, make a declaration in faith: "I will see more in the future than I've lost in the past."

Even the secret petitions of your heart — God's going to bring them to fulfillment.

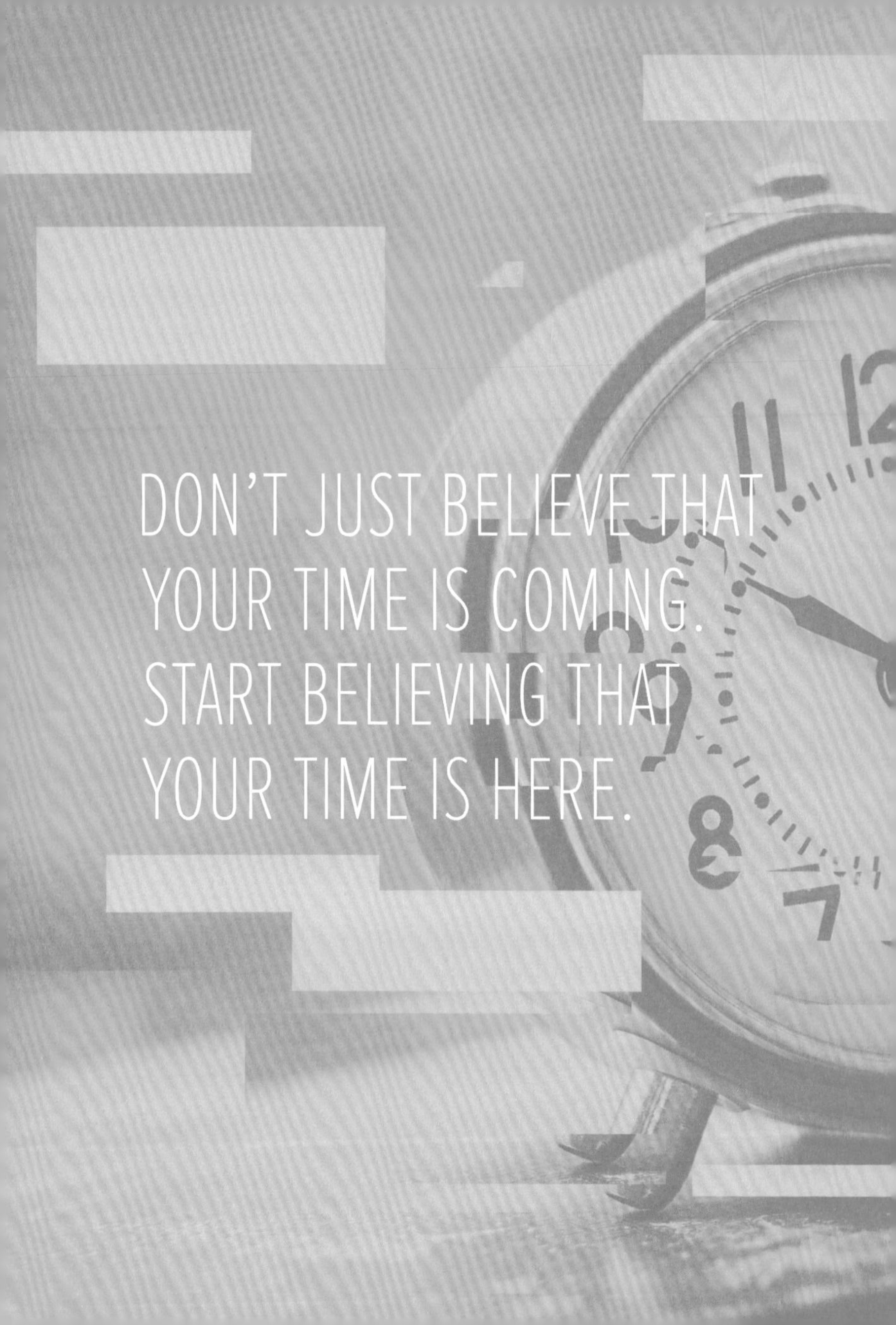

DON'T JUST BELIEVE THAT YOUR TIME IS COMING. START BELIEVING THAT YOUR TIME IS HERE.

IS IT YOUR TIME TO GET OUT OF THE BOAT?

You might be tempted to think, “Joel, that sounds great. I’d love for it to happen to me, but I’ve been through so many disappointments. I just don’t see the point in trying again.” No, the seeds of highest potential God’s put in you aren’t going to take root with that kind of attitude.

You’ve got to rise up and say, “This is my time. I’m entering into a new season, and with my faith, I’m going to ignite this moment. With my faith, I’m going to ignite the dream that’s inside me.”

The Scripture encourages us to fan the flame (2 Timothy 1:6).

At eighty-five years old, Caleb saw his time come. Joseph, after thirteen years of hardship, saw his time come. If God did it for Caleb and Joseph, He can do it for you.

Keep your faith stirred up. Serve others. Give generously. Sacrifice your time.

God rewards obedience, and when you obey, a blessing always follows. If you'll let this seed take root and go out expecting good things, if you'll believe that God is working in your life and that those promises will come to pass, you will see God's goodness in a greater way.

Peter was in a boat with all the other disciples when they saw Jesus walking on the water.

Why did Peter want to get out? Why did he suddenly think he could do that? Because he had seen Jesus open the blind eyes and cleanse the lepers and do all those miraculous things? Yes, that's true, but the other disciples in the boat had seen the same things. Why didn't they want to get out?

It's because Peter understood it was his time. He stirred his faith up. He ignited that moment, fanned the flame and believed he could do what God put in his heart.

And at Jesus' words, Peter stepped out of the boat and walked on the water.

Yes, pretty quickly he sank. He went under, but he walked on the water even if it was only for a moment. Peter walked on the water when the other disciples didn't, and Jesus was right there to help him back up when he fell.

That's the kind of boldness you can have. Don't just believe that your time is coming. Start believing that your time is here and that God will help you every step of the way . . . because He will.

All the dreams that you've buried, those desires that you thought would never work out, it's time to dig them up and start believing again.

You need to have the attitude: "It's my time to come up to a new level. I've seen it happen for others, and it's my time to see God's blessings and favor. It's my time to accomplish my dreams. It's my time to break these addictions. I'm not going to sit around wishing for things to happen anymore; I'm not going to be bitter, hurt or jealous. No, this is my season of increase, of promotion and blessing."

If you do that, in effect, you're saying what Peter said. "God, can I come with You? I believe it's my time now."

Notice Jesus' reply. He didn't say, "Peter, stay in that boat. Don't you know I'm the Son of God?"

No, He supported and encouraged Peter to follow Him out on the water. He responded to Peter's hope that his time had come.

So decide today to stay filled with hope. Don't get complacent and think it's never going to happen.

Even now, behind the scenes, God is arranging things in your favor. Right now, chains of mediocrity, chains of failure, chains of lack and chains of addiction are being broken off you.

It may look like your dream has died, but God can resurrect any dead dream. He did it for Caleb; He can do it for you.

God wants you to live your life with an attitude of hope. And I want you to know, deep down on the inside, no matter where you are in life, your time is coming. Your time is here. Get up every morning and declare it by faith. If you do, you won't be disappointed.

I believe, like Simeon, before you leave this earth, you'll see God bring to pass every dream and every desire He's put in you. He'll pour out His blessings and favor, and you're going to live the life of victory and hope that He has in store!

God has a gift for you today — receive this gift of hope!

GIFTS
OF
GOD
JOY
JOEL OSTEEN

CONTENTS

INTRODUCTION

The Bible says in Proverbs 16:20 (NLT), *"Those who trust the Lord will be joyful."* It doesn't say they might be, or they could be if everything works out. It says "will be."

The Scriptures also tell us that the joy of the Lord is our strength (Nehemiah 8:10).

Toward the end of His time on earth, Jesus told His disciples in John 16:22, "No one can take your joy."

What a powerful statement!

Joy isn't something that can be taken away. It is a gift from God to you and is your strength. Yet joy can also be something we can give away without even realizing it.

It's important to protect your joy every day. We can't control all our circumstances, but we can determine whether or not we have joy.

Even when challenges are in front of you, when you're down and out, when it feels like the world is closing in, God promises He will give you His joy. No person and no circumstance can take that joy away from you.

I pray that you will discover this truth in a greater way as you read the following pages.

Remember, joy is God's gift to you!

CHAPTER ONE

IT'S A DECISION

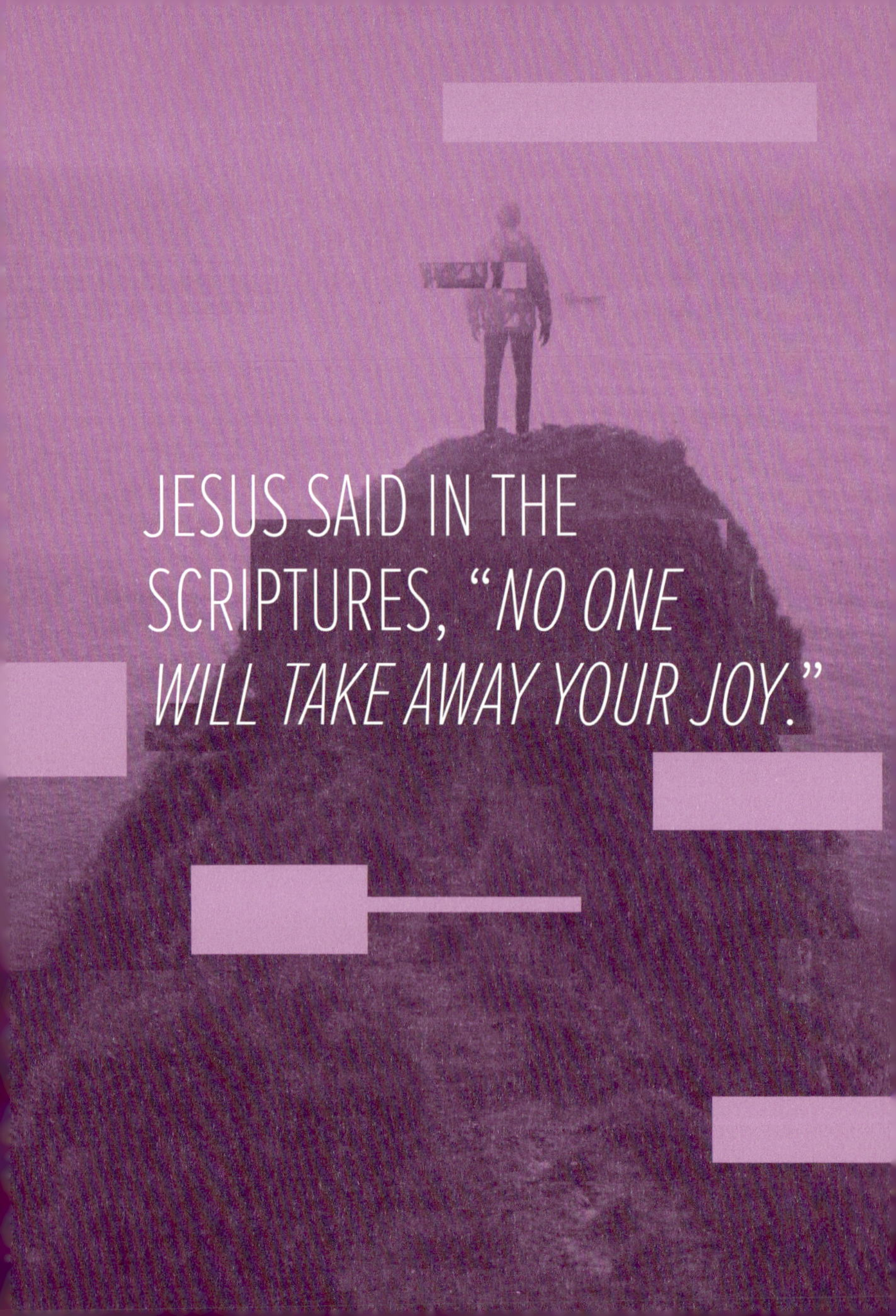
JESUS SAID IN THE SCRIPTURES, "*NO ONE WILL TAKE AWAY YOUR JOY.*"

HAVE THE RIGHT APPROACH

Every day we have opportunities to get upset and live stressed out. Maybe the traffic is worse than expected, your finances take a hit, a co-worker makes your job difficult or a relational conflict arises.

Life can be full of inconveniences that leave you with feelings of disappointment, discouragement and frustration.

To experience joy, having the right mindset and approach in life is so important.

Yes, it's good to have plans, but remember to submit every plan to God, declaring, "God, this is what I would like to accomplish today. This is what I would like to get done. But I know You are in control, so I submit my plans to You. When I make a decision in advance, no matter what comes my way, I'm going to stay in peace and know that You are directing my steps and that all things are working together for my good."

If you'll learn to submit your plans to God and decide in advance to stay in peace, then when things come against you, they won't be a setback. You will have already made up your mind, "That's not going to steal my joy."

I like to pray every morning, "Father, thank You that You've given me the grace to handle whatever comes my way." So when those inconveniences come, I'm ready.

Remember, Jesus said in the Scriptures, "*No one will take away your joy*" (John 16:22, NIV). That means no person can make you unhappy. No circumstance can force you to get upset. It's totally up to you. You have complete control over how peaceful and happily you want to live.

And one of the keys to enjoying life is to take responsibility for your own happiness.

I realize you may be in a difficult situation right now. It may not seem fair. But I want you to know that God has armed you with strength for every battle. He promises to never let you go through more than you can handle. You can experience God's gift of joy in the midst of any adversity.

Jesus put it this way in John 14:27 (AMP): *"Stop allowing yourselves to be agitated and disturbed."* Notice the decision.

God has given you the powerful ability to receive His joy every day.

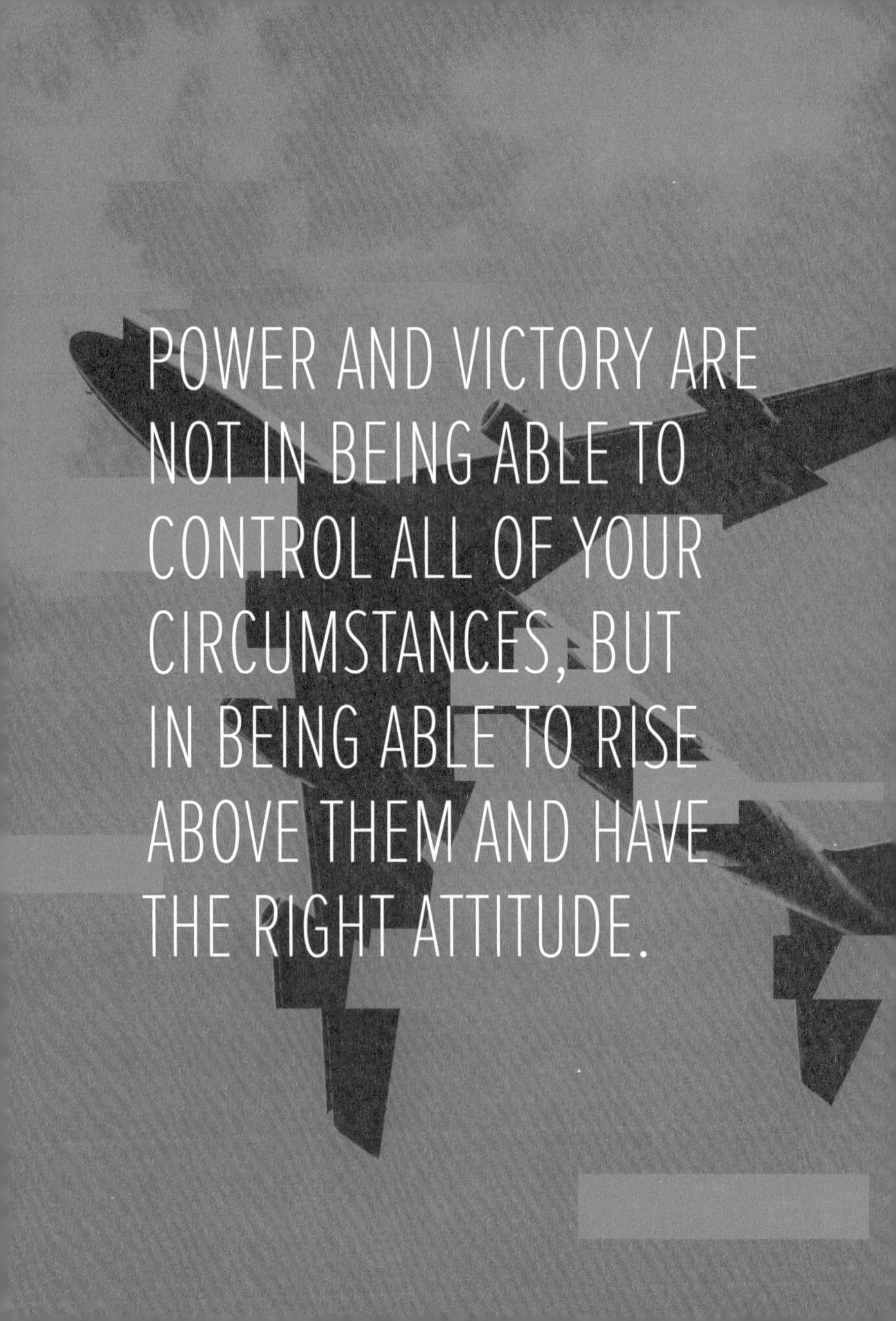

POWER AND VICTORY ARE NOT IN BEING ABLE TO CONTROL ALL OF YOUR CIRCUMSTANCES, BUT IN BEING ABLE TO RISE ABOVE THEM AND HAVE THE RIGHT ATTITUDE.

YOUR SOURCE OF POWER

People tell me, "Joel, I've got a lot of things coming against me." "My spouse gets on my nerves." "My boss aggravates me." "Traffic is horrible." "I'm just under a lot of pressure."

But when I hear them, I listen beyond the words to their heart, and here's what I usually find: The circumstances they describe aren't really the problem. It's their approach — where they've allowed their heart to go. They keep giving away their joy.

If you were to put someone with the right attitude and the right heart in their same situation, they wouldn't be stressed. They wouldn't be uptight. They would still be enjoying their life.

Why? They have the right heart. They know their steps are being ordered by the Lord. They know all things are ultimately going to work together for their good because God is in control.

In other words, they know how to keep their joy.

Proverbs 4:23 (NIV) says, *"Above all else, guard your heart, for everything you do flows from it."*

This Scripture is showing us that our heart is our secret place. Notice how important it is to keep it guarded. If you don't protect your secret place, guarding your inner sanctuary, then frustration, anger and bitterness will flow into your life.

This is why many people have no peace or joy, and only experience discouragement and frustration. It's not that they have more to deal with. It's because they're not guarding their secret place.

Yes, there are things in life you can't control, but be careful not to let those things define you. You can't control the traffic, what your neighbor does or how your boss treats you.

But you can control your attitude and whether you give away your joy. That's where the power lies — not in being able to control all of your circumstances, but in being able to rise above them and have the right attitude.

We all experience unfair situations, but the difference for those who have joy is that they're not letting the negative into their heart.

This doesn't mean you will never feel discouraged, upset or offended. Feelings are a part

of life. But I am encouraging you to not allow those feelings to direct you.

Your feelings will do everything they can to get into your secret place. Worry will knock on your door every night. Discouragement, offense and self-pity won't give up easily. So be determined to say, "No, you're not getting into my secret place. I know God is still in control. He's fighting my battles. I'm not going to live worried and upset."

A lot of times we think, "God, please just change these people who are aggravating me." "God, just make my child straighten up." "God, give me a different job . . . then I'll be happy."

But the truth is, those things should never determine your joy. If you will change, if you will make the attitude adjustment, they won't upset you anymore.

WHAT'S ON THE THRONE OF YOUR LIFE?

What you constantly think about is what you're putting on the throne of your life.

Some people put hurt, rejection or disappointment on the throne. But when God is on the throne, when you choose to declare His Word over every situation, you can be at peace and experience God's gift of joy.

Here's an illustration I like to use: Ships don't sink because of the water around them; they sink because of the water that gets in them. Ships can be in an ocean surrounded by hundreds of miles of water on every side. But that

WHEN GOD IS ON THE THRONE, YOU CAN BE AT PEACE AND EXPERIENCE HIS GIFT OF JOY.

water on the outside, despite the ship's lack of control over it, doesn't become a problem until it gets on the inside.

In the same way, you can't control what happens around you. Bad breaks, difficult circumstances and frustrations may come. The key is to control what gets in you so you don't let it affect you.

Look at these examples from the Bible who used this key . . .

- **The Apostle Paul** experienced shipwrecks, jail time and all manners of persecution from the people he tried to help. Yet he said in Acts 20:24 (AMP), *"None of these things move me."* He could say that because he guarded his secret place. Our goal should be to get to that same place like Paul where no matter what happens, it doesn't move us. Remember, you can't stop the storm around you, but you can stop the storm from getting in you.

- **Joseph** was betrayed by his brothers, sold into slavery and falsely accused. On the outside there was turmoil. He had every right to be upset, offended and bitter. But he didn't let what was on the outside get on the inside. He protected his secret place, operating out of a place of hope, faith, peace and joy.

- When King Saul was trying to kill **David**, David could have gotten angry and bitter and thought, "I haven't done anything wrong. Why is he after me?" Yet David did the same thing we all must do. He didn't let it into his secret place. And just like Joseph, God not only took care of David's enemies, but He also promoted him and took him to the throne.

- Even **Mary**, the mother of Jesus, had to protect her joy. We tend to focus on how amazing Jesus' birth was, sometimes forgetting what she had to deal with. Mary became pregnant while being engaged to Joseph. Can you imagine the talk going around town about her? Mary could have become defensive and bitter, letting the negative chatter get on the inside. Yet Scripture shows us in Luke 2:19 (NIV) that when the angel told her she was going to have a baby, *"Mary*

treasured up all these things and pondered them." She kept God's promises and kept her joy.

You have the power right now to live a joy-filled, faith-filled, peace-filled life. But you've got to come to the point where you say:

"God, even if my circumstances don't change, I'm not going to give my joy away. I know You've got me in the palm of Your hand. I'm totally trusting You."

CHAPTER TWO

LIVING ABOVE YOUR CIRCUMSTANCES

GOD HAS YOU EXACTLY WHERE HE WANTS YOU. IF YOU'LL LEARN TO BE THANKFUL AND FAITHFUL WHERE YOU ARE, GOD WILL GET YOU TO THE RIGHT PLACE AT THE RIGHT TIME.

STAY IN BALANCE

It's so important to realize you can be happy right where you are.

Anything you feel like you must have in order to be happy, might be something that can make your life a lot more difficult.

If you think you have to get married in order to be happy, not only are you in for an unpleasant surprise, but that mindset can also end up working against you.

If you think your boss has to change before you can enjoy your work, you'll go to work every week, year after year, dreading it and thinking it's the reason why you can't be happy.

Always remember: You can be happy right where you are. You can choose to live in constant joy!

I know people who are facing life-threatening diseases. If anyone had a right to be discouraged, it would be them. But they've got smiles on their faces. They're in peace while fighting the good fight of faith.

They're determined not to give away their joy.

You see, it's good to have hopes and dreams. It's good to get up each day believing and expecting for more. But be careful not to wait for those hopes and dreams to unfold before you allow yourself to enjoy life and be fulfilled.

This is the day the Lord has made. Not tomorrow, not when all your dreams come to pass, not when all the negative people are changed. Today!

If you'll learn to be happy where you are, God will get you to the right place at the right time.

And if there is something you really desire, surrender it to God. That's the kind of attitude He's looking for and will bless.

DON'T WAIT FOR OTHERS TO CHANGE

I know a man who struggled in his marriage for years. He and his wife didn't see eye-to-eye on certain issues, and she wouldn't come to church with him. For the longest time, this had him down and discouraged.

Yet when I saw him again one day and asked how everything was going, he seemed to be very upbeat.

He told me, "Everything is going great. I'm really enjoying my life." I thought for sure that he and his wife were getting along better and that

"DON'T BE DEJECTED AND SAD, FOR THE JOY OF THE LORD IS YOUR STRENGTH!"

NEHEMIAH 8:10, NLT

they had resolved those issues. But he said, "No, my wife is just the same. We still don't see eye-to-eye. She still won't come to church with me."

I was so surprised, but then he said something very interesting. "Joel, she hasn't changed, but I've changed. I don't let that upset me anymore. I don't let that steal my joy."

This man had the right attitude and a great heart. His circumstances didn't have to change in order for him to experience God's gift of joy.

Today, you can make that same choice.

You don't have to allow other people to keep you from being happy. Just like that man, you can have joy despite any challenge you face.

WHAT YOU FEED WILL GROW

I realize sometimes we don't have a choice concerning the people who surround us. You may work with someone or live with someone who you feel does things on purpose to aggravate you.

But if that's what you're experiencing, I want to encourage you to change your approach. The more you let people like that upset you, the more you're empowering them. The more you're giving away your joy.

So the next time someone does something that would normally upset you, just stay in peace. Don't give in.

If someone's rude to you, just keep a smile on your face. If someone leaves you out or overlooks you on purpose, make the decision not to let it bother you or steal your joy.

When you rise above those kinds of traps and keep your joy, you're not fueling the fire — you're extinguishing it.

People will tell me, "Joel, I can't help it. They aggravate me. They get on my nerves. It's just too frustrating." No, we CAN help it. The Scripture says, *"You . . . give him power to keep himself calm in the days of adversity"* (Psalm 94:13, AMP).

Here's the key: What you feed is going to grow.

So the next time you get stuck in traffic and you're tempted to get upset, the next time a co-worker is rude to you and you're tempted to let it sour your day, make the decision to keep your joy.

As you stop feeding feelings of heaviness and stress, they'll get weaker and weaker, and eventually, they won't affect you anymore.

Every day when we're faced with choices and situations, it's so important to remember our joy. This gift from God will help us get through the day with victory, understanding that God has a plan and purpose for everything in our lives.

CHAPTER THREE

GUARD YOUR JOY

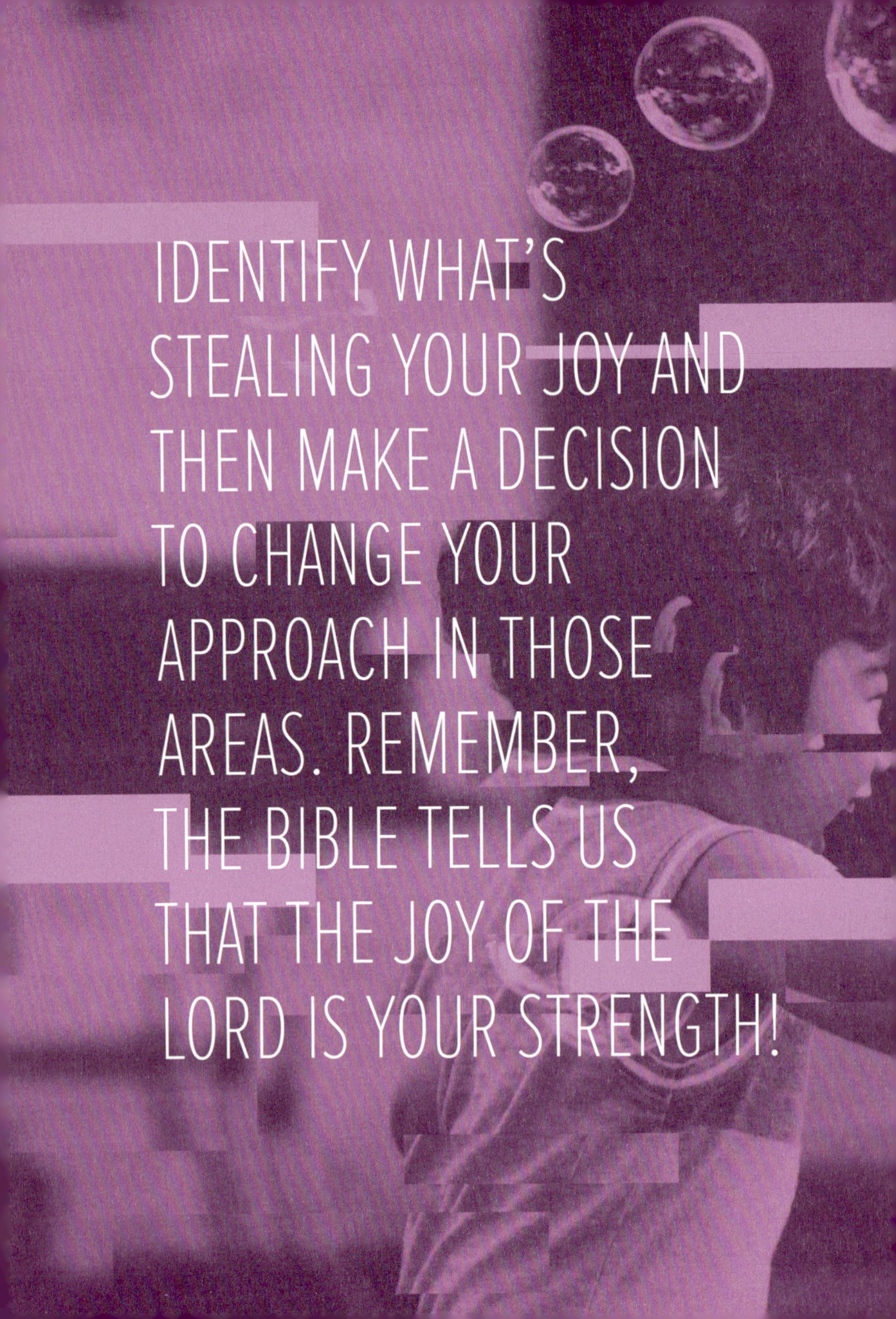

IDENTIFY WHAT'S STEALING YOUR JOY AND THEN MAKE A DECISION TO CHANGE YOUR APPROACH IN THOSE AREAS. REMEMBER, THE BIBLE TELLS US THAT THE JOY OF THE LORD IS YOUR STRENGTH!

IDENTIFY YOUR JOY-STEALERS

How long has it been since you had a good laugh?

I've seen people who go year after year letting the same things upset them. Every time they get caught in traffic, they freak out. Every time their spouse does a certain thing, they lose their joy. If they don't get enough done at work, they come home completely frustrated.

Today, make the choice to have the right attitude. Take inventory of your life and find out what's stealing your joy.

What am I allowing to upset me? What's causing me to go through the day stressed out?

Identify what's stealing your joy by asking yourself questions like those, and then make a decision to change your approach in those areas. Remember, the Bible tells us that the joy of the Lord is your strength!

If you get caught in traffic, getting upset is not going to clear up the freeway.

If someone is rude to you, being rude back to them is only going to sour your day.

If your plans don't work out, stay in peace instead of getting upset, knowing that God is still directing your steps. He's still got you exactly where He wants you.

I remember driving in a crowded parking lot looking for a place to park. A couple came out of the building walking toward their car, and I had to guess which row they were going to be parked at. I turned down one row, and it happened to be the right one. They were parked close to the front door.

I was waiting for them to back out, when all of a sudden, a driver came from the main road, turned the wrong direction to go down that aisle, and beat me to the spot.

My first inclination was to honk and give him a piece of my mind. But I had to decide whether or not I was going to let it upset me. I thought to myself, *I'll give him the parking spot, but I will not give him my joy.*

When you're tempted to get upset, when somebody does you wrong, you have to ask yourself, *Is this worth giving up my joy over? They've already offended me. Am I going to make it worse and let it ruin the rest of my day?*

Some people don't realize they're constantly giving away their joy, and that's the reason why they're not happy.

It's because they gave away their joy. Perhaps it was when they couldn't find their car keys, or when they were in traffic or maybe when they had to work late.

Today, I'm asking you to stop giving away your joy.

Life is too short to let interruptions and inconveniences keep you from being joyful. You might not be able to get away from them, but you can learn to handle them in the right way.

It's so freeing when you understand this simple principle: *I don't have to give away my joy. I can live every day happy if I want to.*

One definition of joy is "calm delight." That means "at peace and at rest," not mad at a spouse, not aggravated at the boss, not frustrated that plans didn't work out. That's the key to living in God's gift of joy.

THE LORD IS DIRECTING YOUR STEPS

Giving up my prime parking spot in the crowded lot isn't what I remember from that day. I chose not to make a big deal about it. After all, a few minutes later I found another place to park.

Then, when I was walking toward the building, a young couple came walking out. They stopped me and told me they had a son in the hospital and that they had been reading one of my books. It was a source of hope and encouragement to them.

"THE LORD DIRECTS OUR STEPS, SO WHY TRY TO UNDERSTAND EVERYTHING ALONG THE WAY?"

PROVERBS 20:24, NLT

The lady began to weep. She said, "Joel, I know seeing you here is God letting us know that everything is going to be okay."

After we talked a moment and prayed, I thought, *I didn't get the parking spot I wanted, but I got the spot God wanted me to have.* God was directing my steps, and meeting that precious couple wasn't a coincidence.

God caused our paths to come together for a reason.

If I had been upset and argued with that other guy, trying to set him straight, I probably wouldn't have been where I was supposed to be.

What's even more amazing is that if I had gotten that parking spot, I might have been well on my way by the time the couple came out of the store. I wouldn't have been able to encourage them, and I would have missed out on what God was doing in that moment.

I understand it can be difficult in the moment, but when your plans don't work out, it doesn't mean you're not at the right spot. If somebody is rude to you, if you're tempted to get upset, just take the high road and stay in peace.

God is a God of justice. He sees every wrong that's ever been done to you, and if you'll keep your peace and your joy, He'll make your wrongs right.

He'll take what you thought was a setback, what you thought was a disadvantage, and He will turn it around and use it for your good!

So always be looking for God's purpose in each situation. There is always something that can steal your joy. I know people who get stressed every time they have to pay their bills each month, every time they have to clean the house or every time they have to work late.

If you're losing your joy from situations like these, now is the time to change. God's given you joy so you can live the life He created for you.

CHAPTER FOUR

YOUR KEY TO HEALTH

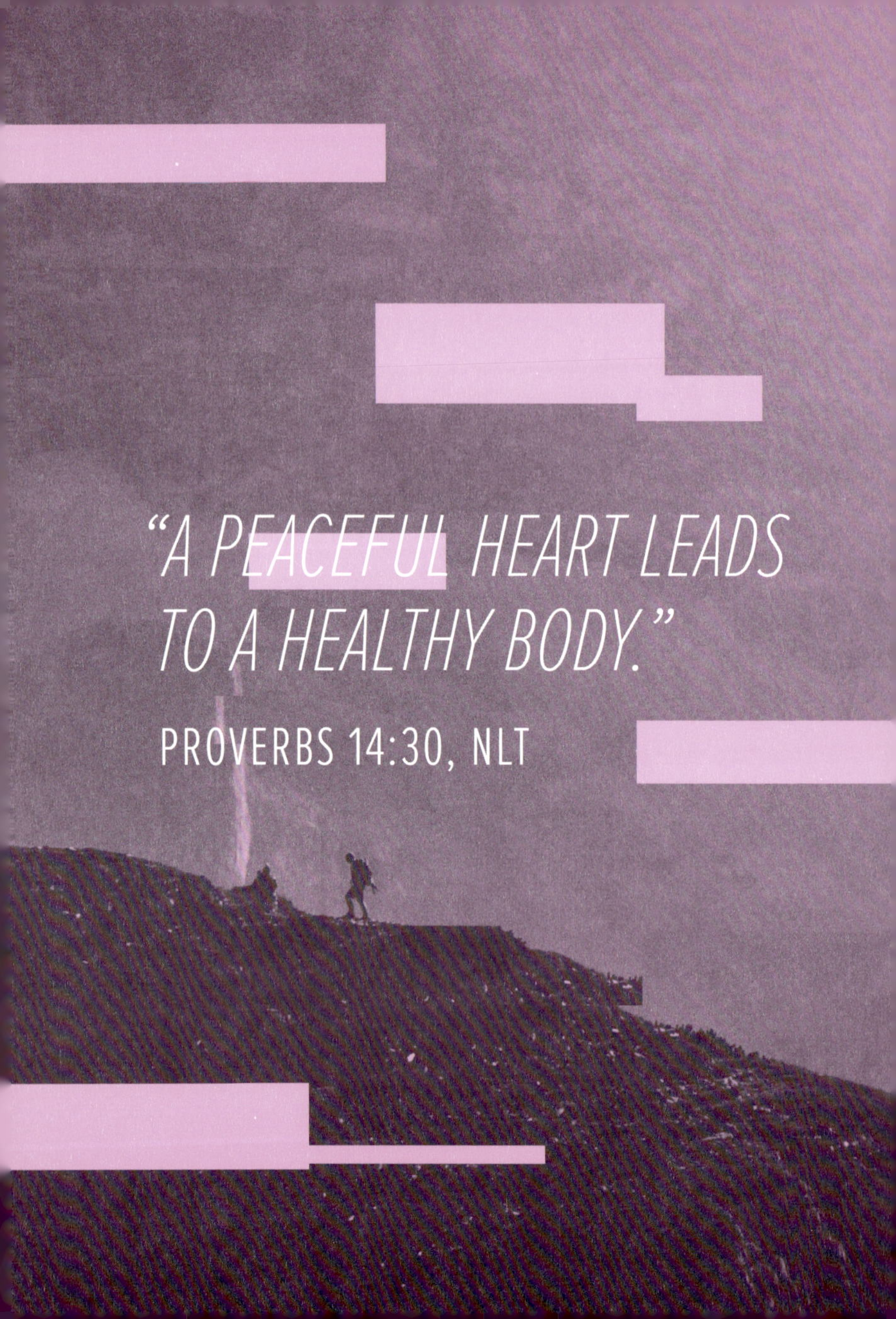

"A PEACEFUL HEART LEADS TO A HEALTHY BODY."

PROVERBS 14:30, NLT

JOY: THE BEST MEDICINE

I've read that there are more heart attacks on Monday morning than on any other day of the week. Why? Because people are uptight and stressed about going to work.

In fact, stress is one of the reasons there is so much sickness in our society. An estimated 60–90% of all visits to a primary care physician are stress-related.

I think we'd be amazed at how much healthier we would be if we'd quit fighting against everything that doesn't go our way.

Remember, God has you in the palm of His hand. Scripture promises that no weapon formed against you will prosper. When you stay full of joy, it's just like taking medicine.

When you're at peace, laughing and being happy, it brings health to your whole system.

The Scripture says it this way: *"A peaceful heart leads to a healthy body"* (Proverbs 14:30, NLT).

I believe many of the headaches, backaches and other ailments in our world would go away if we would stay in a place of peace — not hurried, worried, uptight or stressed out.

Yet some people are always fighting. They're always in turmoil with something, not realizing they are giving away the very thing that could help keep them healthy. They keep giving away their joy.

MAKE THE ADJUSTMENT

I heard about a man who had not been feeling well. He went to see his doctor, and the doctor said, "What's wrong?" He replied, "Well, Doctor, lately I've been getting dizzy, and I'm starting to see these white spots."

The doctor examined him and put him through some tests.

Several days later, the doctor called him back and said, "Sir, I hate to tell you this, but you've got a rare disease, and we think you only have about six months to live."

As a result of the report, the man quit his job and decided to travel the world and do all the things he'd always hoped to do. He spent a lot of time with his family and even bought a new sports car.

One day, he was driving by a famous clothing shop, so he decided to go in and get a tailor-made suit. The tailor came in and measured his arm length, "Thirty-three inches"; measured his waist, "Thirty-two"; measured his pant length, "Thirty-four."

Then he measured the man's neck and said, "I'm going to make you a sixteen-and-a-half-inch shirt." The man said, "No, I wear a fifteen-inch shirt."

The tailor measured it again very closely. He said, "No, sir, you wear a sixteen-and-a-half-inch shirt."

The man was very adamant. He said, "No. I wear a fifteen-inch shirt. I've worn that size my whole life, and I want you to make me a fifteen-inch shirt."

The tailor said, "Well, fine. I'll make you a fifteen-inch shirt. But it's going to make you dizzy, and you're going to start seeing white spots."

I share that story to say that if you're willing to change, if you'll make adjustments, many times you'll see your "white spots" go away. Don't go around with a fifteen-inch collar when you know you need a sixteen-and-a-half.

You'll see the frustrations, and the things that stole your joy, no longer bother you as you make the necessary adjustments in your life and keep your God-given gift of joy.

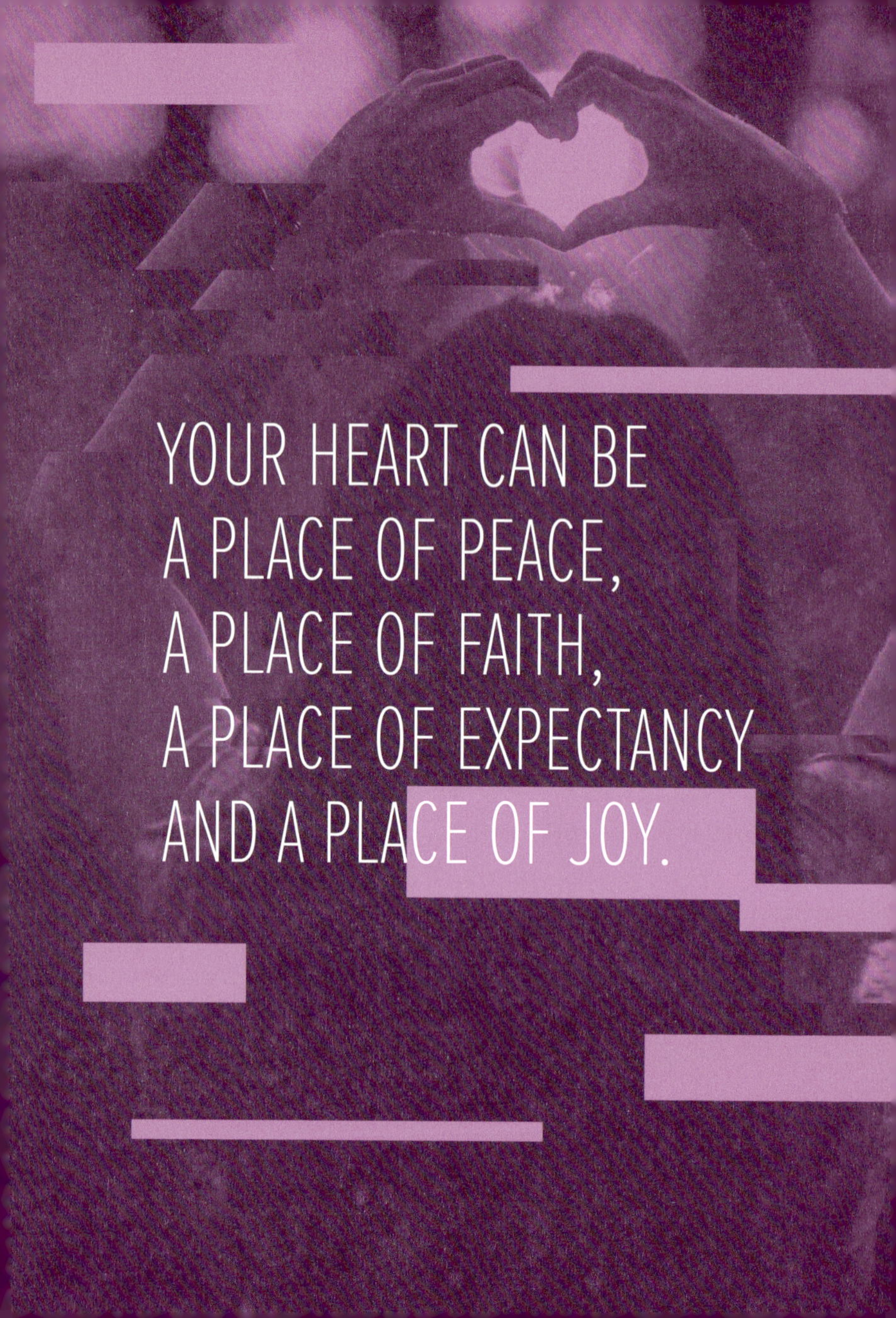
YOUR HEART CAN BE
A PLACE OF PEACE,
A PLACE OF FAITH,
A PLACE OF EXPECTANCY
AND A PLACE OF JOY.

KNOW WHAT YOU CAN CONTROL

Remember, we can't control our circumstances. We can't control what other people do. But we can control our own attitude. That's where the power lies, and when you get your joy back, you'll go to a whole new level.

If you allow other people and circumstances to keep you upset, frustrated and worried, then you'll continue to lose your joy.

But today, if you will make even a minor adjustment and change your approach, you will see a major improvement.

Your heart can be a place of peace, a place of faith, a place of expectancy and a place of joy. Instead of letting the worry and doubt in — like Mary, you can let what God promised you reign on the throne of your heart.

Maybe you're having trouble at work, struggling in a relationship or facing a setback in your finances. Like Paul, you can say, *"None of these things move me,"* because you've got your secret place protected.

So get good at letting things go. Sometimes small things can keep us from God's best. But Jesus said in John 14:1, "Stop allowing yourself to be upset."

If you'll let the small things go, you'll give God permission to show His strength in your life. This is why Proverbs 4:23 says to guard your heart, because small offenses, frustrations — those things can act like poison.

If you'll change your approach and believe that God is directing your steps, if you'll believe you are exactly where you're supposed to be, then you'll come back to that place of peace and hold on to your joy. That joy which comes from God will be your strength.

And not only will you enjoy your life more, but God will also pour out His blessings and favor on you as you live a life of victory!

GIFTS OF GOD

PEACE

JOEL OSTEEN

CONTENTS

INTRODUCTION

Before Jesus left the earth, He told His disciples He was leaving them a gift — *peace*.

Peace lets us know we're making good choices. Peace encourages us and reassures us that we're on the right track, driving away thoughts of worry, fear and anxiety.

Peace is a beautiful gift from God that the world cannot take away (John 14:27).

In his letter to the Philippians, the apostle Paul encouraged the church in this truth.

He told the believers not to worry about anything but instead, to tell God what they needed and thank Him for everything He'd already done.

Yet Paul didn't stop there. He also promised that when they made that choice, the peace of God would guard their hearts and minds in Christ Jesus (Philippians 4:6-7).

Friend, that very promise from the Word of God still applies to you today.

The peace of God will protect you and lead you to your destiny.

I want you to experience this wonderful gift every day because as you discover living in peace and following it, you'll experience the blessings and favor God has for you.

Let go of worry, fear and anxiety. Begin a life of peace today.

CHAPTER ONE

LET PEACE BE YOUR GUIDE

"DO NOT BE ANXIOUS
ABOUT ANYTHING, BUT
IN EVERY SITUATION . . .
PRESENT YOUR REQUESTS
TO GOD. AND THE PEACE OF
GOD, WHICH TRANSCENDS
ALL UNDERSTANDING, WILL
GUARD YOUR HEARTS
AND YOUR MINDS IN
CHRIST JESUS."

PHILIPPIANS 4:6-7, NIV

FOLLOW THE PATH OF PEACE

Too much information, too many choices... these are two common concerns people have in our Internet-infused culture.

With so much information at our fingertips, *how can we know if we are on the right path? How can we know if we are following God's will?*

If you are looking for a way to know if you are in God's will, the presence — or absence — of God's peace is a good indicator.

It is one of the main ways God leads us through life, confirming what He's placed in our hearts.

On the other hand, there are times when we don't feel or sense God's peace.

Something may look perfectly fine. From the world's point of view, there's no reason why you shouldn't do it, but in your spirit, maybe there's an uneasiness. You can't quite put your finger on why, but it just doesn't feel right.

Friend, that is God's gentle way of telling you to wait and hold off.

The Bible says in Proverbs 3:6, *"Seek His will in all you do, and He will show you which path to take"* (NLT).

What does it mean to seek God's will? It simply means before you make a decision, pray and ask God for direction. Then be sensitive and listen to your spirit.

In other words, before you buy that new car, check your spirit. *Do you have peace about it?*

Before you take that new job, before you go see that movie, before you get into that relationship, check your spirit and make sure your decision lines up with God's Word and His will for your life.

If you have peace, then move forward, knowing God is guiding you down a good path. But if there's an unrest or uneasiness, don't override those feelings.

If you will seek God, He will protect you. He will guide you. He will help you avoid trouble and go from good decisions to great ones. He will show more of His goodness in your life.

It's when we ignore those inner feelings that tell us to wait or be careful that we can get ourselves into trouble.

Many people have gotten into a relationship with someone they didn't have peace about and ended up getting hurt and lonely. Others have bought things they didn't really have peace

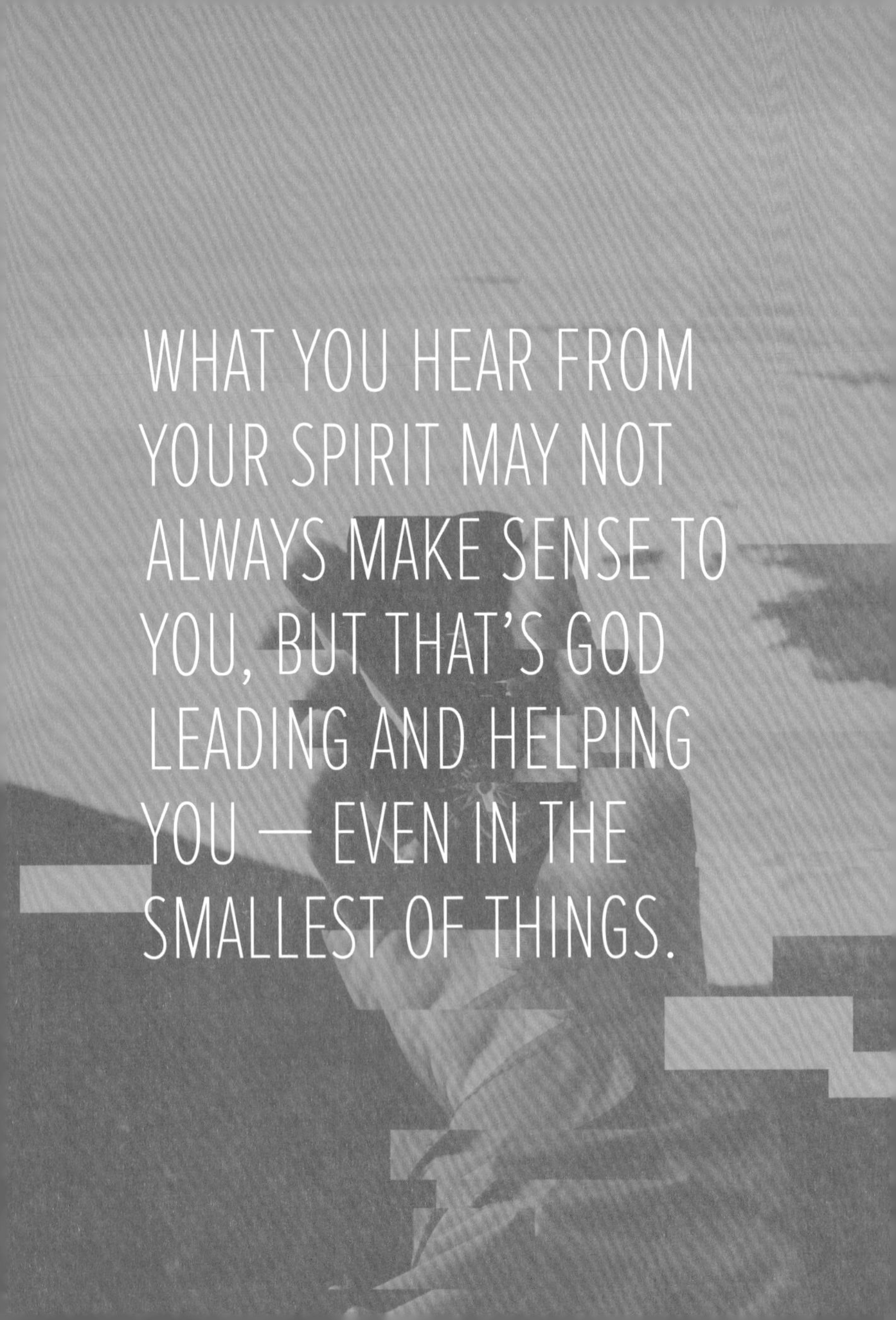

WHAT YOU HEAR FROM YOUR SPIRIT MAY NOT ALWAYS MAKE SENSE TO YOU, BUT THAT'S GOD LEADING AND HELPING YOU — EVEN IN THE SMALLEST OF THINGS.

about and now find themselves in unwanted debt.

But I want to encourage you today that you can hear God's voice. He's given you His Word, the counsel of others, wise people in your life and constant access to Him through prayer.

As you listen to God's voice, you'll start walking in God's will.

LET PEACE BE THE UMPIRE

I like the way the Amplified Bible puts it in Colossians 3:15: *"Let the peace (soul harmony which comes) from Christ rule (act as umpire continually) in your hearts [deciding and settling with finality all questions that arise in your minds]."*

In other words, this Scripture is saying that peace should be the determining factor when it comes to the decisions that we make — just like an umpire, who in sports calls a player safe or out.

So be aware of how your spirit is feeling. If you don't have peace *before* you do something, chances are you won't have peace *while* you're doing it. If you're in a relationship you don't have peace about right now, you're not going to have peace about it later on.

If you don't have peace about buying that new car but do it anyway, then you're not going to have peace when it comes time to make the payment each month.

If you don't have peace about taking that new position but still go for it because it pays more money and has more prestige, you'll probably end up being unhappy as time goes on.

Put simply, it's so important to learn to follow God's peace. It's one of the key ways He desires to lead you.

HELP IN THE SMALL THINGS

One day I was at the mall and found a tie I wanted. I'm kind of picky when it comes to certain things, so when I find something I like, I normally don't think twice before buying it.

But just as I was about to go up to the counter and pay for it, I felt an uneasiness. I don't really know how to explain it. I just didn't feel right. All of a sudden, I knew with certainty that I was not supposed to buy that tie.

In my head, it didn't make any sense, but because I've learned to trust my spirit, I didn't buy it. So we left, and just as we were about to leave the mall, we stopped by one more store.

Not only did they have the same tie, but it was also on sale for almost half the price!

Here's why I share this story with you: What you hear from your spirit may not always make sense to you, but that's God leading and helping you — even in the smallest of things.

You're not always going to know why you have an uneasiness, but if you'll learn to just trust your spirit and follow what you're feeling on the inside, you'll go down the correct path. That's the Holy Spirit leading you.

A family member of mine tells the story of when he was going to buy a new SUV. He is a very detailed and thorough buyer, so he spent several weeks researching and trying to find the best price possible. Finally, he made his decision.

He had everything lined up — the right color, the right model, the right price — but just as he was about to sign the deal, he suddenly didn't feel peace about it. He felt uneasy inside and decided to put the deal on hold.

Several weeks went by, and I noticed he hadn't made the purchase yet. I asked him, "When are you getting your SUV? What's taking so long?"

He said, "Well, Joel, the truth is, I just didn't feel good about it, so I put it on hold." I said, "Really? Why? Was it too much money, or you just couldn't get the right model?" He replied, "No, none of that. I simply didn't have peace."

From the world's point of view, it was odd. He'd done all this work and was so excited about it. But what's interesting is, about a month later, a dealer called him back and said that the manufacturer had just put out word that they were offering a $5,000 rebate to anyone who purchased one of those vehicles.

All of a sudden, he knew why he had felt that uneasiness and why he didn't have peace prior to now.

He could have overridden how his spirit was feeling. He could have done his own thing and bought the vehicle. In the same way, if we'll learn to follow peace, God will show us more of His favor. He will cause us to be at the right place at the right time.

Today, he not only has a new SUV, but he also has an extra $5,000 he can use or give as a faithful steward of God's resources.

There's no telling how many times God tries to bless us like He blessed my family member. There's no way we can know how many times God tries to protect us and keep us from danger.

Today, let's start following the lead of God's peace.

CHAPTER TWO

TRUST YOUR SPIRIT,
TRUST GOD

DON'T TRY TO FIGURE EVERYTHING OUT. JUST TRUST YOUR SPIRIT. THAT'S GOD SPEAKING TO YOU, AND HE ALWAYS HAS THE BEST OUTCOME IN MIND.

RECOGNIZE GOD'S VOICE

Many times I hear people say, "Well, I wish God would just speak to me. I wish I could make better decisions." Or, "I just wish I had clear direction for my life." But the truth is, God is speaking to every one of us.

Job 33:14 tells us, *"For God speaks again and again, though people do not recognize it"* (NLT).

So often, we're waiting for this voice to boom out of the Heavens, telling us what to do.

Yet most of the time, that's not the way God speaks. Instead, He speaks in a still, small voice. He speaks through His Word. He speaks to us from the inside, through a peace, a rest and knowing His voice.

This is how the Apostle Paul heard from God. He said in Romans 9:1, *"With Christ as my witness, I speak with utter truthfulness. My conscience and the Holy Spirit confirm it."*

He was saying in effect, "I don't have to see three visions to know what to do. I don't have to hear five trumpet blasts. All I have to do is pay attention to how I feel inside. If I have peace, if my conscience is clear, if there's a rest in my spirit, then I go ahead and do it."

In the same way, you don't have to make hearing from God and staying in His will some difficult, super-spiritual thing. You just have to learn to follow your spirit.

If you take a step of faith and still have peace, then keep going.

But if you start to lose your peace, be wise enough to back up and wait until you feel good about it again.

We need to make checking our spirit a habit — something we use on a regular basis.

DO IT GOD'S WAY

My dad tried building our former sanctuary about five years before it was finally able to be built. He'd get up in front of the congregation, excited, and say, "This fall, we're going to start our new sanctuary project."

Then fall would roll around, and he would get back up there and say, "You know what? I don't have peace about it. We're not going to start yet."

He tried to start it probably four or five times on his own timing and in his own way, but when it came down to it, he followed his spirit and listened to the voice of God. He knew if he did it without peace, he wasn't going to have God's anointing, and it was going to be a constant struggle.

But right before Christmas one year, in practically the worst recession Houston had ever experienced, he began feeling peace about the sanctuary project. That's when he knew he was supposed to start.

From the world's point of view, it was the worst possible time. His friends told him, "John, you're never going to raise the money in this kind of economy. You might as well forget it." But he felt peace on the inside, and he followed his spirit.

Sure enough, the sanctuary was built debt-free in a little over a year.

Just because you know you're supposed to do something, just because God's put the dream in your heart, doesn't mean the dream will follow your own timing. You've got to follow God's gift of peace.

Don't expect to always understand why you feel a certain way. Don't try to figure everything out. Just trust your spirit.

God is speaking to you, and He always has the best outcome in mind.

GOD SEES THE BIG PICTURE

You may meet someone new at work or at school, and she seems like the nicest person in the world. Everybody likes her. She's kind, friendly and outgoing.

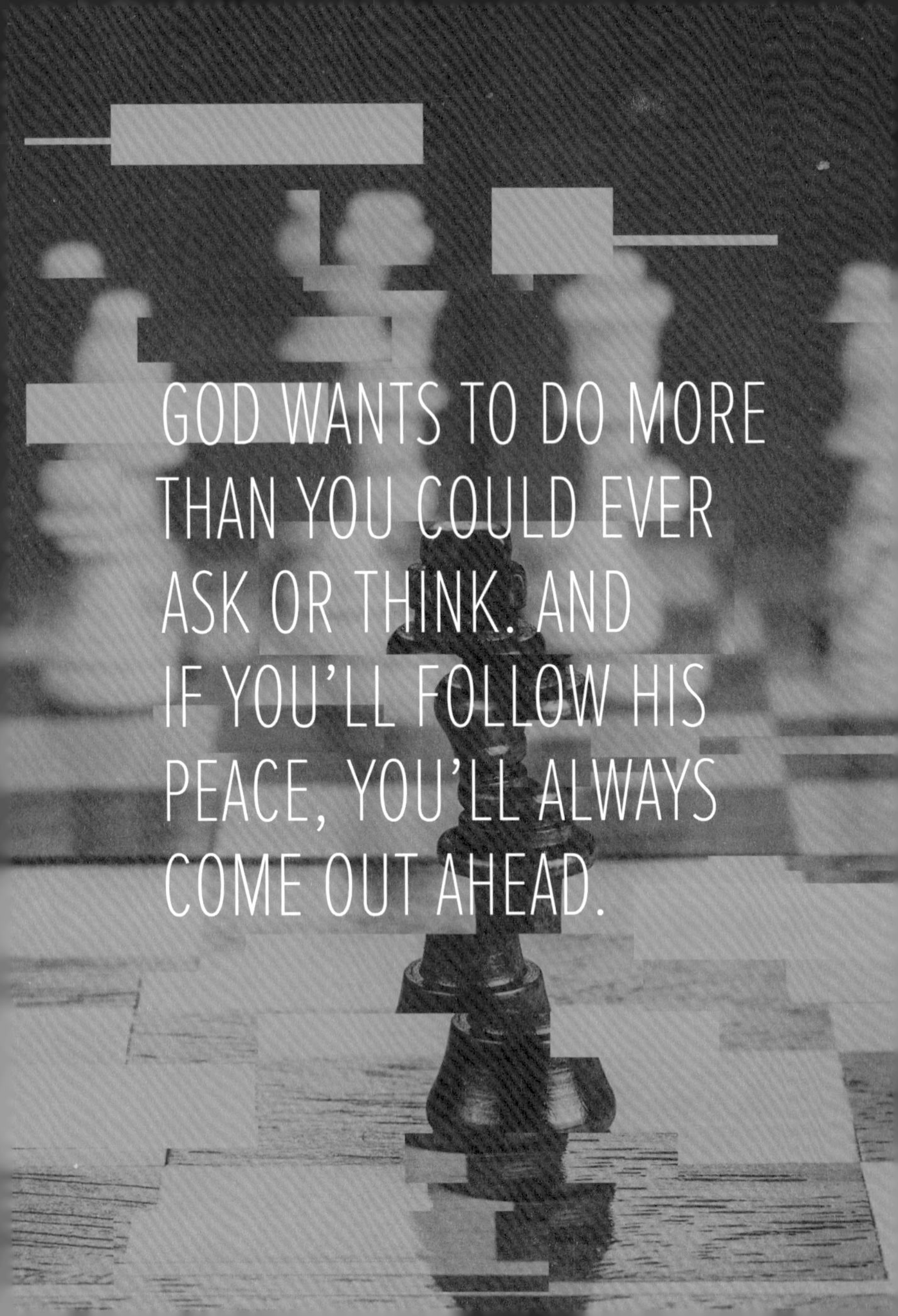
GOD WANTS TO DO MORE THAN YOU COULD EVER ASK OR THINK. AND IF YOU'LL FOLLOW HIS PEACE, YOU'LL ALWAYS COME OUT AHEAD.

But it seems like every time you're around her, you feel this uneasiness, and you don't know why. Something just doesn't feel right. Your head is telling you, "Hey, lighten up; quit being so sensitive." But your spirit is telling you, "Be careful; watch out; there's something wrong."

That's God's way of saying back off and be careful.

I've heard so many times, "Joel, he's perfect for me. He's good-looking. He's outgoing. He makes good money. He's friendly." And all of those things are great, but *what are you feeling inside?*

If there's unrest or uneasiness, don't override and ignore it.

I've seen too many people end up getting hurt because they continued in relationships they didn't have a peace about. They tell me, "Joel, I always felt like something just wasn't right. From the very beginning, I didn't have peace about this relationship."

Remember, God knows what's best for you. You can only see a little down the road, but God can see the whole path. He can see the big picture for your life.

God knows when there's a dead end around the corner that you can't see.

Don't get so caught up in your emotions and the excitement that you override the uneasiness He's placed in your spirit.

I've seen people, every time the alarm goes off on the inside, push the uneasiness down again and again and again. In most cases, they do this because they want their own way.

They don't realize that God's ways are so much better. But here's an important truth: He's not going to make you do what's right. He will give you those warnings. He will give you suggestions. He will take away your peace. But He won't force you to do the right thing.

When God says no, when you feel that uneasiness and you're not really getting your way, it's not because God's trying to make your life miserable. It's not because God wants you to go through life lonely. It's simply because God has something so much better in store for you.

God wants to do more than you could ever ask or think. And if you'll follow His peace through your spirit, you'll always come out ahead.

Instead of trying to make things happen on your own, follow the peace of God into all the amazing things He has for you.

CHAPTER THREE

SEEK GOD IN EVERYTHING

IF YOU WANT TO STAY IN GOD'S BEST PLAN FOR YOUR LIFE, I PROMISE HE WILL HELP YOU. HE WILL LEAD YOU THROUGH HIS GIFT OF PEACE.

CHECK YOUR EMOTIONS

It's so important that we not make emotional decisions, especially long-term ones.

I've seen so many people get caught up in the excitement of the moment, overriding the uneasiness they are feeling.

But God is not going to yell at you in those moments. If you will acknowledge Him, He will help you to make good decisions; He will direct your path.

Imagine that you're out for a nice, leisurely drive one afternoon, and you decide to stop by a car dealership and take a look at some of the new vehicles. Sure enough, the longer you're there, the more that desire starts to grow in you to buy one.

Your emotions get all stirred up, and you think, "I need one of these. It's my favorite color, and if I buy it today, I get a free barbecue grill! It's a sign from God."

Meanwhile, an alarm is going off in your spirit. You're feeling that unrest. God's still, small voice is saying, "Don't do it. You can't afford that. Don't make an emotional decision."

How many people today are under a heavy burden of debt because they bought things they didn't have peace about in the first place?

It could all be avoided if we'd just let God lead us with His peace.

Anytime we have to make a decision when we're excited and our emotions are running high, I think the best thing we can do is just step back, take a break and wait. If you can, sleep on it a couple of nights. Pray about it and see how you feel on the inside, in your spirit.

If you want to stay in God's best plan for your life, I promise He will help you. He will lead you through His gift of peace.

GOD KNOWS WHAT IS BEST FOR YOU

This reminds me of the story of a young lady who is a gifted singer. She has an incredible voice, and her dream was to one day be in full-time ministry.

When I first met her, she was working at a professional company as the marketing director. But one day, out of nowhere, she got a call from one of the largest and most prominent ministries in the country. They offered her

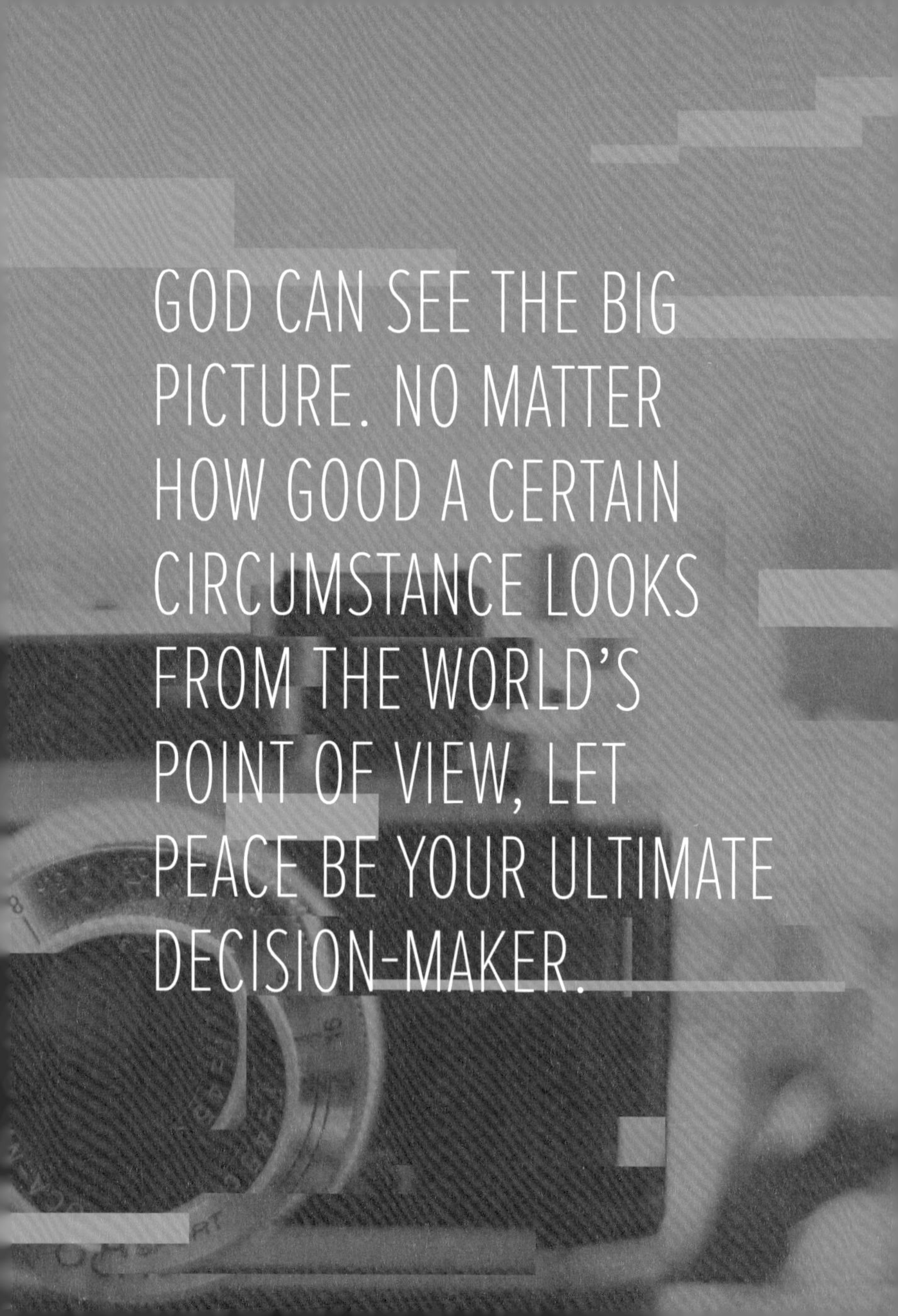

GOD CAN SEE THE BIG PICTURE. NO MATTER HOW GOOD A CERTAIN CIRCUMSTANCE LOOKS FROM THE WORLD'S POINT OF VIEW, LET PEACE BE YOUR ULTIMATE DECISION-MAKER.

a full-time position to come help lead worship for their ministry.

Not only would she be singing to thousands of people in auditoriums across the world, but also through the television outreach, she would have the opportunity to impact an even larger audience with her gifts. It was a dream come true.

She and her husband went out and celebrated that night. They were so excited; it looked like God had done more than they could ever ask or think. They told the ministry that they would get back with them in a week or so and let them know their final decision then. But during that week they both began to feel an unrest.

From the world's point of view, it was a no-brainer. They should accept it. But deep inside, something didn't feel right.

The husband felt especially strongly against it, but he thought it was probably just his nerves about moving to another city. After all, this was his wife's dream come true. He didn't want to dampen her enthusiasm, so he just kept it to himself.

Then a couple of days later his wife came to him and said, "You're going to think I'm crazy, but I don't think we should take this new position. Something just doesn't feel right." He began to explain how he had been feeling the same way. They told me that when they made the decision to decline that offer, it was like this heavy burden just lifted off of them.

All of a sudden, they got their peace back.

From the world's point of view, it looked like she was passing up a once-in-a-lifetime opportunity.

Yet what's interesting is that several months later, that ministry was involved in a big controversy. The ministry eventually ended up laying off more than ninety percent of its employees.

If they had accepted the job, they would have packed up their family, moved across the country, quit their good jobs, taken their children out of school, bought another house, and found out it was a mistake.

But after that experience, God began to open up door after door. She ended up recording many albums and having a very successful career.

I share that story with you because I really want you to get this truth deep down into your heart: God knows what's best for you.

God can see the big picture. No matter how good a certain circumstance looks from the world's point of view, let peace be your ultimate decision-maker.

TIMING MAKES ALL THE DIFFERENCE

One time in the Gospels, Peter went out to go fishing. A few other guys joined him, and they fished all night but didn't catch anything.

The next morning, Jesus came along and said, *"Throw your net on the right side of the boat and you will find some"* (John 21:6, NIV).

And sure enough, when they did, they caught so many fish that their nets began to break.

There's an important spiritual principle to this story.

When Jesus came along and gave direction, everything changed! Jesus, in essence, was saying: "If you will do it My way, if you will let Me lead you and guide you, you'll begin to see great things happen in your life."

As Peter obeyed, he experienced firsthand the abundance and blessings of God.

In the same way, when you learn to acknowledge God, following what you're feeling in your spirit and doing life His way, He will take you places far beyond your dreams!

CHOOSING PEACE OVER WORRY

Inevitably, you're going to be faced with the choice to follow worry or peace.

This happened to the Israelites in Exodus chapter 14.

God had just delivered them from slavery. They were headed toward the Promised Land, and life was good. But on the way out, Pharaoh changed his mind about setting them free. He and his army came chasing after them and wanted to bring them back into slavery.

The Israelites looked up and saw horses and chariots coming at them full force. They were at a dead end at the Red Sea — they had nowhere to go. It looked like they would certainly be recaptured or even killed. They began to panic, and fear spread through the whole camp. The Scripture says they were terrified.

They said, “Moses, why did you bring us out here to die? Weren’t there enough graves in Egypt?” Moses knew if they would have stayed upset and worried, their unbelief would cause the Lord to stop working on their behalf.

So Moses said to the people, “Don’t be afraid, for the Lord will fight for you if you hold your peace and remain at rest.”

Again, notice the decision.

Experiencing what God had for the people of Israel didn’t come by worrying. It came from peace. And the same principle applies in your life today.

Always be careful not to be led by what you feel — such as worry or fear — but be led by your spirit and the peace God gives you.

CHAPTER FOUR

LISTEN TO GOD'S VOICE

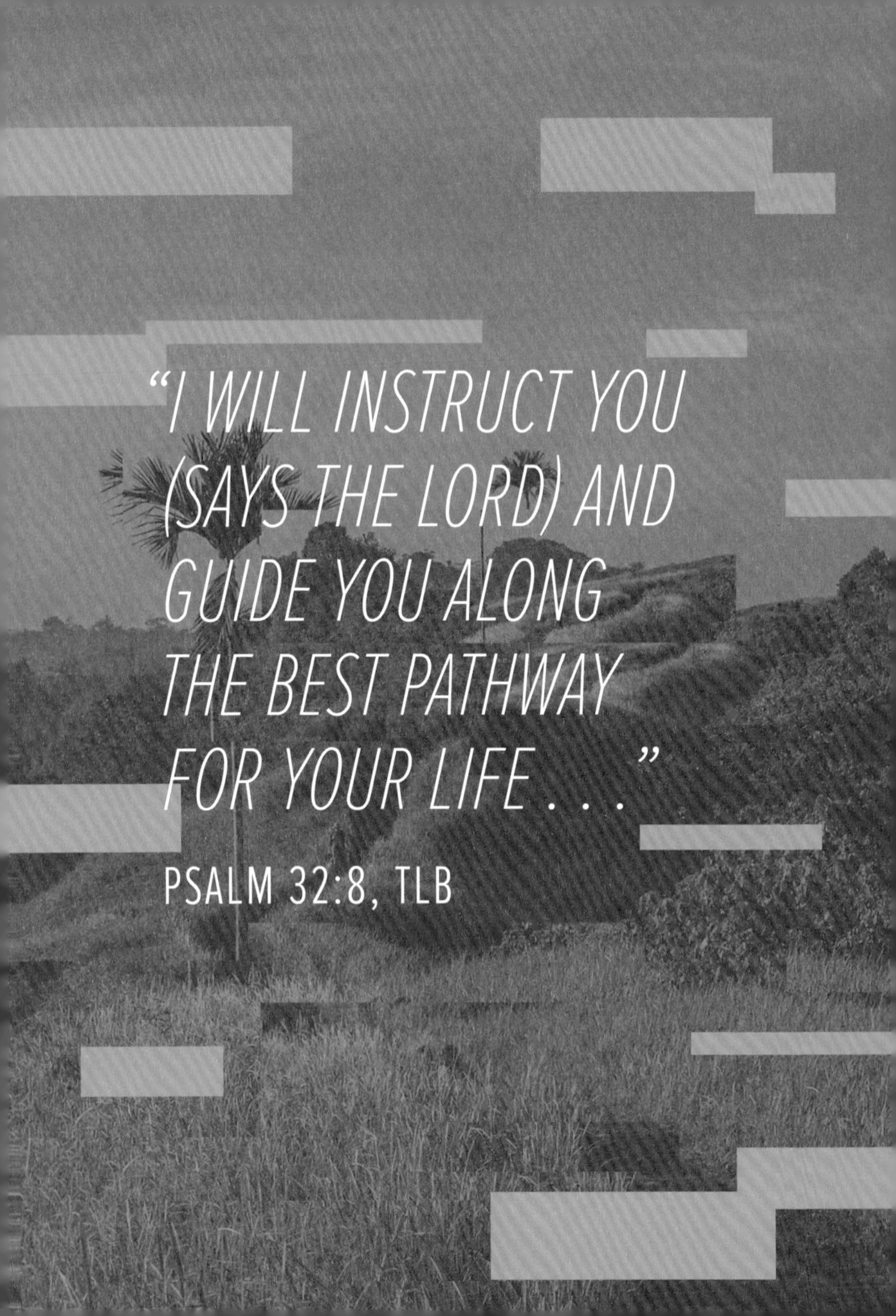
"I WILL INSTRUCT YOU (SAYS THE LORD) AND GUIDE YOU ALONG THE BEST PATHWAY FOR YOUR LIFE . . ."
PSALM 32:8, TLB

SOMETHING WAS WRONG

It's so important that you pay attention to the still, small voice on the inside. Don't ever do something if you don't first have peace about it.

I think about the time in the Old Testament when Isaac was a very old man. He was close to death and wanted to give his son, Esau, the blessing that belonged to the firstborn.

Isaac was basically blind; he couldn't see anything. One day he called Esau in, and he said, "Son, if you'll go out and kill some game and prepare me a meal, I'll give you the blessing that rightfully belongs to you."

Esau's mother, Rebekah, heard this. Because she loved her son Jacob more than she loved Esau, she told Jacob to go put on Esau's clothing while she made Isaac his favorite meal. She then gave it to Jacob and sent him disguised as his brother Esau to see his father.

"Dad, here I am. I've got the meal you asked me for. Now you can give me your blessing."

It's interesting how many times Isaac felt like something was wrong throughout the story, but he just kept overriding the warnings.

He replied, "Esau? How did you get back so quickly from hunting? You've never prepared a meal for me this fast before." Notice the alarm went off. Something wasn't right. He felt that uneasiness.

Jacob made up an excuse. "I don't know, Dad, it just all fell into place. Everything worked out just right." But Isaac still didn't feel right.

He said, "Well, come over here, Esau; let me make sure it's you." Since Esau was very hairy,

Jacob had put on some animal skins so he'd feel like his brother. Isaac thought to himself, *Well, it feels like Esau, but the voice still sounds like Jacob.*

God warned him again and again, but Isaac ended up missing it just as we miss it so often.

He went ahead and blessed Jacob even though he didn't have peace. He went against what he was feeling in his spirit and blessed the wrong son.

So often, we fault Jacob for being a deceiver — and certainly he was wrong — but God tried to warn Isaac. Right before he mistakenly blessed Jacob, he said once again, "Tell me the truth. Esau, is this really you?" Notice his lack of peace.

When Esau finally came back in with the meal he had prepared, and Isaac realized what

WHEN YOU FOLLOW
THE HOLY SPIRIT'S LEAD,
YOU'RE GOING TO
EXPERIENCE THE BEST
GOD HAS FOR YOU.

had happened, he said, "Esau, I've made a terrible mistake. Your brother has tricked me. I've given him the blessing that belongs to you, and I cannot take it back."

Esau said, "Dad, surely you can do something. Surely you can bless me as well." He said, "What's done is done."

And what a shame — it all could have been avoided if Isaac had just listened with his spirit and not with his ears.

GOD WILL GUIDE YOU

I heard a story about a man who was a well-known pastor. He was a sought-after speaker all over the world, and his ministry was growing.

One day, he had a speaking engagement in another city, and the next morning he was to get up and catch a flight. The night before, he woke up in the middle of the night with a very distinct unrest and uneasiness on the inside. He knew something wasn't right. He tossed and turned, unable to go back to sleep.

The next morning, the first words out of his wife's mouth were, "I just don't feel good about you taking this trip today."

These weren't pre-flight jitters — this man had been flying around the world for years, and this was the first time he'd ever felt something so strongly, and it was the first time his wife had ever said anything like this.

He began to explain to her how he had been feeling exactly the same way the night before.

What they felt wasn't fear. There's a difference between fear and having a lack of peace. What they felt was a lack of peace.

Unfortunately, the man followed the example of Isaac. He overrode all the warnings. He thought, *I can't disappoint these people. I promised them I would be there. It's been scheduled for a long time, and I just can't let them down.*

He overrode his conscience and went against what he was feeling in his heart.

Tragically, that plane in perfectly good weather had a rare problem and ended up going down. Not one person survived.

Afterward, his wife bore witness that God tried to get their attention. He tried to warn and protect them, but they didn't follow peace.

Now, I'm not trying to bring fear on you. I'm not saying that if you get nervous, don't leave your house. I'm just sharing with you about the importance of following your spirit.

Don't ignore the uneasiness or warnings you feel on the inside. Listen to that still, small voice and follow God's peace.

EXPERIENCE PEACE EVERY DAY

My dream is that you would experience the abundant life God has in store for you. But I know that all starts when you make good decisions.

So always let peace be the umpire, and follow your spirit.

The Scripture says in Psalm 32:8 (TLB), *"I will instruct you (says the Lord) and guide you along the best pathway for your life . . ."*

When you follow the Holy Spirit's lead, you're going to experience the best God has for you.

David had all kinds of opposition and enemies coming against him. He could have lived upset and worried constantly. But he declares in Psalm 23:1-2 (AMP), *"The Lord is my Shepherd . . . He leads me beside the still and restful waters."*

He was saying, in effect, "I don't focus on my worry or fear. I focus on God and am led by His peace."

Remember, God knows where the favor is, and as you're sensitive to His voice, paying attention to what you're hearing on the inside, there's no limit to where He will take you.

God will show you more of His favor, and you will experience the amazing life He destined you to experience.